STONE   WIND   WATER

STONE
WIND
WATER

POEMS

David Lee

Rainshadow Editions
Black Rock Press
University of Nevada, Reno
2010

ISBN 978-1-891033-50-6

Library of Congress Control Number: 2010924706

Printed in the United States of America

The Black Rock Press
University of Nevada, Reno
Reno, NV 89557-0224
www.blackrockpress.org

Cover painting, "Long Shadows" by Susu Knight

for

Tom Auer
Ken Brewer
Ellen Meloy
Leslie Norris

Vayais con los dioses
Os quiero

Contents

Autumn   Wind   Song   70
Autumn Koan   71
Stephen Dedalus on the Slide Guitar   72
Frost Warning   73
Thornapple Aubade   75
Requiem   76
Equinox   Novena   86
Sabbath Year, Insomnia   88
November Idyll   89
Windburst   90
Cold Snap   92
Nocturne   Chinle Strata   94
Tumbleweed: an Autumn Portrait   95
Moon of the Hummingbird   97
Moon   Wind   Owl   99

4

Idyll   102
Cold   Star   Wind   Sonatina   103
Matins in the Cathedral of Wind   105
Wild Rose Nocturne   114
Turquoise Elegy   110
Eventide   112
Thornapple Nocturne   114
Desert   Moon   Star   116
Wind   Sand   Moon   Arch   117
Mind Drift: Neolithic Sliver Moons   119
Century Plant   121
Dark of the Moon   124
Winter Solstice   125
Solstice, Midnight   128

Coda: Winter   Morning   Shaving   129

Notes   130

One generation passeth away, and another
generation cometh: but the earth abideth for ever.

—Ecclesiastes

With our thoughts we make the world.

—Siddhartha Gautama

The heaven and the earth and all in between,
thinkest thou I made them in jest?

—Quran

It is interesting to contemplate an entangled bank, clothed
with many plants of many kinds, with birds singing on the
bushes with various insects flitting about, and with worms
crawling through the damp earth, and to reflect that these
elaborately constructed forms, so different from each other,
and dependent on each other in so complex a manner, have all
been produced by laws acting around us...There is grandeur in
this view of life, with its several powers, having been original-
ly breathed into a few forms or into one: and that, whilst this
planet has gone cycling on according to the fixed law of grav-
ity, from so simple a beginning endless forms most beautiful
and wonderful have been, and are being, evolved.

—Charles Darwin,
The Origin of Species

Notes Toward the Autobiography

Four turns of the prayer wheel:
        sharp air striking the face
        blue sky
        golden-red sand
        the globe of fire wandering above

and a fifth from deep time:
        the clutch of ancient seas,
        eons gone, pulls against my knees

ONE

*Try to paint the world as though you are the first
man looking at it—the wind and the heat and
the cold—the dust and the vast starlit night*

—Georgia O'Keeffe

*Far in the east
The gods beat
On thunder drums*

—Alice Corbin,
The Green Corn Dance

*While the music of the spheres may have been
discounted as scientific fact, it remains a theory I
am unwilling to part with.*

—Modean Gill

Aubade Paean
Fanfare for the Uncommon Man

   —after Aaron Copland

   A soft spot
   in the cloud rips

   Streamers of light
   spill and
   glister the buttes

   until the cloudseam heals
   Then the redarkening
   around dawnseep

   trickles through
   a notch in the horizon

   A piñon
   stuffed with song

   joyance
   of white-crowned sparrows
   A crepitant windchime

   erupts
   into a geyser
   of quarter notes

   fills the sky

   Glory

                    —for Leslie Norris
                      1921-2006

                    I

Behold

—Milton, *Paradise Lost* I, 777

A wonder
the mind of God
to see
not
the tiny
dark seed

but
living
inside it
the magnificent
lemon scented
white blossom

2

Ghost Dance at Arches

A Lilith moon's half ghost,
goddess of the neaps,
flareskirts the fenestrated mesa,
a white mussel fossil
above trundled clouds
shimmering from the backlight

First breeze
The cuesta asleep,
curled into the cave
of its own dream,
a soft movement
like the tug on the mind's reins,
desert a glass bowl, golden,
skimmed with dust

Clouds flex and mumble,
shove the winds before them
as they begin their pour
over the scarpland,
a tsunami untethered,
ready to scour the bajada basin

       ★   ★   ★

Creosote branches
claw the storm's bellyfur,
bend and rive
half uncials in sand

Night collapses upon itself
as dark wind
rips a slash through black sky
with a gnarled finger
Stars' splattered embers
kindle like a lost
fragment of lightning

The gash opens
to moon firedamp,
St. Elmo's light through the sandstorm
on the ancient sea's floor,
an ocean's manes rises
from its crypt, glides

★   ★   ★

A lever of dawnseep
on the fulcrum
of Moab sandstone
pries the dark to unearth
radiant copper

Crisp windy morning
crosses over a billowing
green sea of creosote

ravel of bird waltz and moon drift
like the rustle of waves
pulling away from tule grass

Fugue
Sunrise   Tea   Kitchen Table

What call'st thou solitude, is not the Earth
With various living creatures, and the Aire
Replenisht, and all those at thy command
To come and play before thee?
  —from the on-line journal of John Maestro Beloved

All night it seemed quiet
until just before dawn

a cricket chir-chirruped
a cicada thrumsisked

a kangaroo mouse scuttled
from the cupboard across the kitchen

its tiny feet thricking on saltillo
the ceiling stretched and crackled

the wall creaked its contrapuntal answer
the saucepan boiled a bobolick bod dob

the water sisished into the mug
the teabag paflumped its belly out

the dog sasdalloped the insides
of his bowl and it claklitit the floor

the mahogany leaves rasheeted the wind
the dry leaves kashie kashied

then a jay cursed and a crow
clacked and khawed and a robin

said *donde* and a hummingbird
phummed its invisible wings by the feeder

and a lost goose *awked* above the house
a meadowlark tee tee weefee *teewhee teewheed*

the rosefinches and sparrows *djueed teedleeted*
around the grainbowl all their songs

growing wings and flapflapping their way
into a sky stuffed already cramfull with sound

Provo Canyon, Equinox

—for Kitty Norris

The river
smug
with the secret
knowledge
of gravity

thunders
froth and spume

its roar
spits up rainbows
bright as
crushed mint

shatters
over
drowned boulders

the flagellant delirium
of willow
and sawgrass

then smooths to mirrors
of cloud flecked indigo
held in place
by the utter stillness
of golden aspen

sunlight's purl
tangled in mist drift
swallows

knife through ripe shadows
thick and heady
as stout ale
on god's breath

or dark knots
of shaggy rock
ringed pine
smoke

Wind Psalm

Sand wisps
thin and pale
as a ghost's shadow

under a freighted protestant sky
heavy with the faith of wind,
laden with the guiltweight of dust.

Braids of wind swirl,
thicken the air,
cling to each other.

Dust saturates the sky,
glides on a path
of sundrenched wind,

rests inside the brittle edges
of curled four wing
saltbush leaves,

drips in a thick duffel
across the salt domes.
The cross breeze

trapped in sandstone bowls
lunges to root itself
beneath the arroyo lip,

slinks like a chuckwalla
into a slickrock fissure.
Wind touches every spine,

feather, hand, hoof, stone,
eye open or closed,
petal or leaf,

the desert wrapped in wind,
shaped by its gesture,
clothed in dust.

Everywhere the sigh
of dust drenched wind,
the breath of God

moves over the flesh
and shadow of God,
the whisper

of the sacred
upon the body
of divinity.

Crows Laughing at Thunder

Beethoven 6: 3

Clouds shape and reshape themselves,
wind around a silk tendril
of hidden thunder,
the echo of a cello or a siren
sings in the language of trees,
manzanita, afternoon rain.

A bright meadow gash
the color of the mountain's heart,
firecracker penstemon and gentian
frame a gnarl of woodrot and burl,
fecund behind the tangle of root ball.
The secret scent
of a moist wildflower
honeyed wind

braids with the agate fragrance
of mountain shower.
Through the rain
the sudden flash and ozone blister.
A small eternity after radiance,
before it touches skin, earth

leaks the croak and gurgle
of a ribald coffle of crows,
storm drunken in the sixty foot
scrape and groan
of lightning branded yellow pine

The great rumble
collapses before laughter

like a child's unearned guilt
caught and held on a nail
hammered into sky,
shatters into ten thousand bright bits
wafting like confetti above a brass band
down upon the storm strafed loam.

Rhapsody for the Desert

In the *Kama Sutra*, erotic sounds are said to
come in seven categories...I have heard all
these in water.

—Craig Childs, *The Secret Knowledge of Water*

Himkara   *nasal release*

All afternoon the mating hum
and drone of cicadas,
their conjoined hanging
in the cottonwoods like Blake's angel,
celebrate the turbid intimacy of wind
and water, the survivance
of sunflooded bajada, tree and sky,
a momentary liberation

Hush of dusk,
interval of twilight silence
seeps over desert,
sinks into earth,
broken by the sonidas de la noche,
the courtship bullroar
of a nighthawk's wings
throbbing against quarterlight,
nasal *peent* slicing the air

Stars in pear blossom clusters
so bright the sky's branches
bend with the weight of evening
push forward to
a reemergence of cicada chorus,

sky retreating deep
into the color of night

Beside the La Sals a moon
bright as a sego lily
frozen in blue ice

      Stanita   *great, loud release*

Thunderlight,
the sky callused
with knots of storm,
the smooth bowl of horizon
clings to gnarled clouds

a sudden burst of wind
and blinding scream,
great boom and rumble
pushes the air aside
to rush ahead
like a young dog
following musk
room to room

sour fragrance
green as ozone
on a cloudless day

crushed sage scent
of muddy river,
the Colorado twenty miles away

        ★   ★   ★

bellow as great boulders
uncleave the canyon wall,
bolt free
then shatter,
crack and shout
as giants fall through sky
tumbling like pinecones
as they drop,
all

      ★   ★   ★

frost and sun bloom,
Landscape Arch sheds its skin,
underbelly peels away

as if sky turned
to exfoliating stone
blossoming in air

scaffolding of earth
compound fractured

explosions of breath and dust
as the half life of arch
bursts against shattering ground

the swollen hollow
looms

      ★   ★   ★

the release

the embracing silence

Kujita   *hiss of escaping breath*

Over scarp and mesa
a billowing silk curtain
of walking rain,

shimmer
in milky blue
moonlight

An eddy of wind
sifts through
a sandstone gap

No horizon
only dark blur
where earth and air merge,

fade to evening
Breeze and a small rain
embrace

pulling the tether lines
of creosote and cholla
until they sigh

like scuttling steam
before the chubascito
curls into a fist

Slung rain
sizzles as it
strikes slickrock,

arroyos gather,

muddy water
moves downward,

slot canyons whisper
as if filled with snakeskin
slithering over sandstone

The sky stills,
salted with stars
and no voice of cloud

Burrowing owls
nod and bob
before their den,

bow and chatter
until a nightshadow
crosses

From within
             chicks rasp
and rattle

like the hiss
of wind
moving through dried leaves

Lac burnished
on thin creosote fingers
Pale slanting moonlight

Sutkrita *gentle sigh*

Dark of the moon
over Navajo sandstone

heavy clouds
and summer monsoons adrift,
so still the creosote
do not breathe

In a tinaja
a perfect reflection of sky

Pegasus drinks
near a floating dipper

milky way flotsam
edges the basin like foam

as if a god
had tapped

against the bright
bowl of night

a shard split off,
tumbled to slickrock

and slid with a gentle sigh
to its dark pool

Phutkrita   *violent burst of breath*

In hollows
between butte and midnight
a pale scratching of fingernails
on the spine of silence
as a new moon scrabbles,
pulls its way upward
into the black mirror of sky

A trap door opens
with the push of a falling star
A ravenous wind drops
through the stone breech
from a point of light,
falls with the mind
of its own geometry

whips, swirls, lunges,
now a spiral,
its own self-reproducing
incestuous search
through tunnels of night
narrow as snake paths
in cheat grass

enters a canyon,
gully, arroyo,
                a chute
brings its own intense hunger
and the promise
to tear its way out

scours the bones of the earth
seizes what it can clutch
carries as far as it is able
then tosses it aside in a mad frenzy,

climbs the scarp
and screams in a violent burst of breath
as it leaps out of the gorge,
vanishes like memory
into the labyrinth of distance

slot canyons gargle
sharpened wind,

gravel beds steam,
datura breathes

the bright glisten
of wind scoured sand

Dutkrita   *single painful cry*

A mooncurve
of phosphorescent cloud
dangles above the oncoming storm,
a windripped scar
on the closing sky

       ★   ★   ★

The dark thunderhead
drags lightning

across the desert
like a child breaking
a pig to leash,
screams heard for miles,
great cumulus gathered
into a black knot,
its neck swollen with frenzy

*   *   *

Clouds open
and flap their wings
of thunder

*   *   *

An earth shuddering explosion
loosens rain and wind

Juniper limbs whip and struggle
in the lashing rage

like a tethered hawk
flailing against the scream

of gravity's deathclutch
Storm plunges into desert

*   *   *

Sudden snap as a cottonwood
tithes a great limb
to the chubasco

Shattering roar

then as quickly
the silence

Rush of water

      ★   ★   ★

Like a maul's scream
driving a splitting wedge
deep into the belly of night
a rain wakened Woodhouse toad
bellows its painful cry,
a single bleat
overarches the tilting moon,
all the world's love and hurt
in one call
falls on the stretch marks
of arroyo and stone
scoured and riven
by the spring drench,
dissolves to whisper,
murmur of breeze,
leaf quake

          ~

Scent of crushed desert lavender
A cricket calls to the moon

      Rudita   *soft weeping sound*

Thin night air
whispers the stars apart
at the equinox horizon,
distances them as they rise
until darkness brims
with flickering light

The voluptuous Pleiades harem
lorded by Taurus
low in the night sky
Soft unanswered sob
of a mourning dove

Shy Orion,
a self-conscious toe
scratching reticence
into whorled sandstone
answers separation
with opulent silence

Canyon call
of a spotted owl
cooo-weep

La Llorona wanders
the narrows
her sorrow
echoed in the slot shadows

drifts always away
and down
into the murmur
of moving water

a love song

rises like
the mind of the moon,
starlight raining
through the dark

then silence,
a grace note
carved in sky

Remnant

being the remainder of a carved down pretentious son-
net on the Michelangelo effect of wind, including a joyous
horse and a gorgeous arch, both unanticipated before being
stumbled upon while wandering

A wind gust
             wallows
in an arroyo,
             rolls,
then rises and shakes its mane,
leaps
       to trample a rabbit brush
huddling on the lip.

Suddenly
this crimson framing arch,
wind's triumphant joy,
the majesty of sandstone
frozen momentarily,
a grand pas de deux,
in its slow sojourn
·back
to bright dust.

Equinox   Siesta

A mirage is the desert dreaming
about the ocean who used to live here.
—Baucis Rojas

I

The desert yawns and sprawls,
laden with sky,
flecked red on gold

the memory of snuffed starlight,
its belly shimmers
a Monet canvas

Warm air
over cool sand
lifts a small cloud

in the sun-slick sky, its shadow,
like Beethoven changing moods,
shoves its way along

2

A quivering mirage
pushes light up the mesas
through shadows
hiding in flutes
into sky

where it glistens the air
like scattered jewels
seen through a mirror

Suspended horizon
a breaching narwhal
above this out of place sand and stone landscape
up for the bright air

delicate and fragile as the memory of spindrift
clinging to a bare strand of light,
tethers the dissolving cloud tatter
to the blue crevice of mesa wall

3

In the bajada
clefts of tangled basalt
like fallen moon shards,

a wind riven salt dome
still as the scar
of a dried river

Light and time
pooled in stone basins
beneath sky

mimick the stillness
a coyote snuffs
and knows as death

4

A cactus wren calls
through air thin as dream,

scent of juniper
thick as blood

A beardtongue nods with the weight
of a pollendrunk bee

The old sun rolls,
the earth turns in half-light

Moonrise   Sandstone   Waterseep

—after Henri Rousseau

The moon
sprawled across the belly
of a sandstone dune

sky shimmer

Night
fragrant and moist
over
the ossified desert

unpins its dark hair

with a shake and quiet shrug
lets it fall
across the shoulders
the secret archways
of horizon

float into moondrift

Above the dreams
of buried stones
the glitter of a red-spotted toad's tracks
through slickrock
the shining waterseep

darkness closes

stars low on the rimrock
like a crouched cat's eyes
trained on bajada

the joining
the embrace
again

—for Jan, with love

Spring   Storm   Alone
Ode for Walpurgis Night

—after Mussorgsky

Demonic winds howl
and shake their locks

Gnarled cumulus fingers
stretch like nightmare,
clutching slivers of lightning

a sift of thunder
chokes a small canyon
with the leakage
of shrill echo

The swollen sky flares,
a sacrificial angus bull
sucking wind,
nose ring tethered to Factory Butte,
its angry pull loosens
every chink and buttress
in the bajada scaffolding

Sand flays the cuesta
in small, sharp bursts,
scuttles into hollows,
out and around fins
like an enraged weasel
snarls and snaps

searches to confront any object
perceived as affront or impediment,
at every turn screams triumph

* * *

A rumble,
the cloud flings its arms outward,
sheets of rain
with a rich man's love
only for possession
pound the desert
in a fusillade

scars of stones
scoured and slashed
in the black drench

Storm dips
then pours itself
a devil's tithing

Arroyos rumble with slurry
Pellets of rock, grit, fine sand,
a swaddling of red dust
fills the badlands

The bellow of lightning
freed from the mildewed
crevice of underworld
frames an out of place ocotillo
clawing the air like a forsworn proselyte
caught in the wind shear
between fact and opinion,
bloodied fingers slue in freefall

* * *

The sudden break

moan as an eddy of wind
sieves through a sandstone breech

gurgle and croak of moving water

soft thunder
like draft horses
shifting weight in night stalls

fat clouds, farrowed,
hover

The desert shimmers
with the glisten
of a spit shined enigma
unencumbered
from a loose pocket of night
balanced in the open palm
of a sure fulcrum

A spadefoot toad
glued to a pothole lip smiles,
a tiny Buddha
singing in perfect
trochaic trimeter

As in a Vision

these clastic dikes
godplowed terraces

taprock
blind corrals

where half
past bedtime

the wind lay
on a moonquilt

down
to sleep

amidst the waft
of peppergrass

when spring winds cease

almost

unnoticed they pass
like the memory

of a not
particularly
welcome visitor

who
forgot to come
(uninvited) to
the dinner
party

and wasn't
missed: by
any

one

Cactus Wren   Nocturne

Sunset pours
from a cleft

smooth and glistering
the satin blossoms
of a prickly pear
surf

break over
ledges of air

A baritone trill
iridescent
as mist rivulets
trickles

down fluted cliffs
of wind

soaks up
the eastern mesa

behind which
a new planting moon
hides her nakedness
in pools of darkness

TWO

What a glorious world Almighty God has given us. How thankless and ungrateful we are, and how we labor to mar His gifts

—Robert E. Lee

Wherever you live is your temple

—Buddha

Neap Light

A curl of light
descends the bajada

like a raft of pelicans
with luffing wings

blown off course,
intent and deliberate

in its low slide
over a slickrock sea

then with the nonchalant shrug
of an overlooked beatitude

pours itself
into the liquid darkness

of canyon

On the west wall
a desert phlox

hides in its soft cushion
between two shafts

of red sandstone,
glitters

in the thin windwashed light,
silent and pensive

as Botticelli's Venus, the lavender scent
of a Guadalupe altar virgin

or a mewed anchorite
beneath a pale cloister of sky

wedged in matins

Matins: In the Moonset

between timelessness of light
pouring through the holy land

of eternal space
and distant heartbeats of low tide
and neap

fog like sacred smoke
crawls up
from the canyon
spreads

> *a claret cup*
> *its blossoms red*
> *as a sibyl's voice*
> *or a monk's robe*

sings
to the crawling sun
stretch of horizon
dark habited clouds in procession

as they ascend like prayer

point past themselves
to the prophetic confluence
of anticipation and destiny

Starlight's jewels
glisten on the spread petals

Slot Canyon

In the desert there is all and there is nothing.
God is there and man is not.
—Balzac

Great smooth stanchions
vault like a slow gesture
across a corner of sleep

The mind's eye rises
to easy invitation
by the memory of sky

Twisted slickrock
tightens inward
gnarled roots tethered in sand

A moonflower huddles
in eternal shadow
against the nave wall

A blue collared lizard blinks
then closes its drowsy eyes
beneath a white blossom

One seamless furl
rock to sand to leaf
to body to white petaled next

As if the desert
turned itself inside out
to contain this moment

Drought Reverie

It's still a story without an ending
—Rick, *CASABLANCA*

I

South wind
a furnace drought

Sky ready to collapse
under the weight of its emptiness
thermals flatpressed
against the desert
clouds stuffed beneath horizon

cracks in the caprock
elbow and jigsaw their way along
divide the mesa's hemispheres
like a cobweb disarticulated

ribbons stream and drop away
into the filtered glowlight
of fissure and slot canyon

where wind and oncewater
intensified the winter
of considerable discontent
against any concept of permanence

Great rocks lean inward
their scumbled shapes and shadows
their phyletic memory
contoured by erosion
and the mysterious knowledge
of gravity

2

The cleft's yawn
reveals a shadebaked subway

rising trill
and waterfall echo of canyon wren
like the burble
of rushing crystal

a fugue
heard in one of the mind's
distant arroyos

3

A dark line of cloud
bites into sky

hurls itself downward
from the north

a jeweled necklace
flung

4

Fisher Towers rise
and glow

their bright edges sparkle
in early dusklight

slice the swirling winds
into quadrants

A small cloud dances
about the pinnacles

a sailboat
tugging against its mooring

The sky's tides
ebb with the updip slope

of waning moonrise
horns tilted erect

5

Movement like thought
or spilled water
spreads slowly

follows the patterns
of its own gravitation

a story
ready to spiral earthward
or sprout wings
and lift

into its hidden meaning

July Whirlwind

A black and gold
and brown
and green and white fletched
banty rooster
scratches in the dust
like a devil
who will take on
any adversary
with red eyes and long spurs
and raised hackles and a bright comb
that can make
even a subaltern deity's
soul sweat

—after Wallace Stevens

Solstice: Sky   Sun   Bird

> There is a muscular energy in sunlight corresponding
> to the spiritual energy of wind.
> —Annie Dillard

(Dithyramb: from the heavens the clear notes of a ferrugi-
nous hawk, *kree e ah*, followed by the choric echo off a dark
bluff wall trails across desert floor, drops into canyon: *kree e
ah   kiar ah   chiar os*)

Strophe
He who does not prefer form to colour is a coward.
—William Blake

Chiaroscuro.
Pale Vermeer light hovers at the edge of horizon
like a shy suitor long at the curb,
begins a stumble
                and slow climb
down the mesa
traces a finger over an incline,
a boulder's edge, up a tree trunk,
its branch
gathers balance
                jaunts across bluffs
vaults an arroyo
slides over the knees
of darkness and shadow

falters at the desert floor
spreads like a tinctured mist
into the lurch of sage,
rock cleft

46

wanders like a sleepy owl
skyblind and dayshy
into the Sargasso pools of gulch
                              and canyon
floats and quivers
as the rock begins its blossom

Sun stretches,
flexes and spreads,
scallops the desert floor

into ripples of light,
shadow,
gnarled grasp of creosote

dwarf lupine and larkspur
scattered
like chips of sky

A robin, as focused
as one of Bosch's disciples,
kicks the flensed and light-gilded
juniper detritus
                  eddied
outside the rim of dark tree

a small rustle
              grand jete' in miniature
like the waterfall
in a canyon wren's morning song
dances inside puddles of shadow

A world turned back on itself

a bright wind
vibrates under deep blue sky
its lunar tides leaping strong
billows the furls
cascades of light

sunrise on cholla
the burning bush
unconsumed

eager threads of white sun
                                squirm
through holes
in the juniper tangle

a dry gulch
                a fallen strand of light
caught between the banks
dangles above the shadeponds

Antistrophe

Hail holy light...
Bright effluence of bright essence increate.
—John Magnificent, PL, III

Out of a hollow sky
a wall of pouring light
baroque and blazing
scatters music before it
in a great wave
unspooling from the spheres
transformed into feather and wing

shaped
into the language of geometry
by cactus flower horizon
mesa, arroyo, piñon,
creosote, four-wing saltbush, sego lily,
primrose, blue grama

imbued by the texture of shadow,
the lavender moisture
of invisible breathing cloud

the reds and browns of ferric oxide,
chlorophyll green of photosynthesis,
pinks, purples, crimsons
and yellows of fertility

sweet pollen scents
honey the air
lift rhythms of birdsong
into crevices of breeze
                        and light

Cliff swallows
swoop like fighting kites

their chatter
squeaks the rusty light

A rough-legged hawk's whistle tumbles
like a stone
                or the memory of a fallen god
wings clench
like a folded fist
shattering the air

thirty two feet per second
                            per second
toward a point on the desert floor
moving
        836 miles per hour
around the earth's axis
spinning
        in orbit circling the sun
64,800 miles per hour
in a solar system flowing
                    in its ellipsis
43,200 miles per hour
focused, all
            by a patch of light
wild and rapt as an El Greco martyr
crashing 186,300 miles per second
on a tiny ball of fur
                    scuttling
hellbent for shadow
its tiny kangaroo mouse heart
                            races

712 beats per minute

the scarlet mesa sanctified
bloodied like an altar

Indian paintbrush, Eaton's penstemon, scarlet gilia
streuseled rabbit brush aflame
horizon's fringe a prayer shawl
sun climbs into the longest sky

Epode

> Thus the light rains, thus pours...
> The liquid and rushing crystal
> beneath the knees of the gods.
> —Ezra Pound, Canto IV

The roar and dash of light
its jaunt and bound

tumbles about, ebb and flow,
spray, mist, splash and pool

flings the air into troughs and waves
waft and plunge
crests sparkle like a child's shout

on the finger
a painted lady butterfly

light warp of bleaching thunder
shatters the chitin of darkness

Two fork tailed barn swallows
lifted out of a Brueghel's dance
stitch the glowlight
on thin lines
            tethered
to the earth's heart
pas de deux

A daylight moon, gibbous,
humpback jorobado god of luck

or Kokopelli fluteplayer of fertility,
bellringer of the heavens
wanders
      out of place
            pale and ghostly
an evening primrose suspended in sky

Morning pours
with the sweet scent of sapphire
through wisp and dawnlight

A freshly kindled wind
skips through jeweled beardtongue and snowberry
fluttering like hummingbird wings,

pauses, as if a carved gesture of mist
off trail and momentarily frozen:

a single sego lily blocks
the pathway to canyon

Light wrestles the desert
like Jacob's angel

pins it down
until the crow shouts its name

limps through gorges
on a hollowed thigh

cluster of rock and shadow,
shapes the maze of inverted echo
the heating, cracking, exfoliating,
falling of red sandstone

ricochet of ancient trochee, anapest
thermodynamic peel, peal

goatfoot birdfoot forward
the light falls the earth turns

tic clomp tic clomp
tic clomp

(Exode: a red-tail hawk in the high grasp of a slowly pirou-
etting thermal. A husk of sound wafts earthward: *keer*.)

Mutant Haiku at Ground Zero
Yucca Mountain, Nevada Test Site

An altar for a desecrated burnt offering
human sacrifice
to a god of non-existence, blind and deaf

Death of a Small Thing

Battering winds
shear the gunwales
of cloudlet
into silver flay strips

White foamed
flotsam
brightens
the sinking sky

Sonatina   In The Space

between two mesas
red-winged blackbirds

six in the green palm of juniper

above the graveled floodrace
high-banked

glisten
in the sweat soaked nakedness
of afternoon sun

o-ka-leee

        ★   ★   ★

a cactus wren
chug-chug sings
in the skeleton
of an abandoned piñon

braided river of bees
works the claret cup

rustle as wind
wanders
the gulch

sweet song of golden light
tumbling
over a mirage dreamed lattice of sea
hanging in the foam
of three quarter day

*   *   *

a huge orange moon
balanced
on the stretched index finger
of a cholla
rimrocked
on the horizon
poor-will

Duskwind   Fugue

Alles nahe werde fern
—Goethe

A piñon coaxes
the scapegrace lilt
of wind sough

like the suck
of a hoof
lifted from tankmud

a quiet nicker
trickles its way
over soft lips

the print
slowly pulses
with seep

a spadefoot toad
struggles upward
into the tiny pool's center

the scent of moonrise,
the clamor
of love cries

a solitary vireo,
its slow water music
hidden

inside
the grace note windshimmer
of fragrant piñon

Chiaroscuro: Limning Dark Canyon in B Flat

> Coming out of the canyon is an unforgettable
> experience, with all the deep mountains sitting
> mysteriously around and so much sky.
>   —D. H. Lawrence

Opus One

Pellucid light
a silver aureole
around the moon

Opus Two

The strike
of light

shaping
the Bears Ears'
vertical edge

its glistering
steep
in the sheen

the refulgence

Opus Three

The landslide of night
The blackshining sky
The winds

hard pressed against earth
The small explosions of stars
quivering in their sockets
The owl call
a dark tonic
from the refugium
sheathed in the artifacts of time

Opus Four

Smooth stones
polished
by the moon's tides

Opus Five

A dry creek
runs through sand
and stone

The moon
like a hawk
swoops
over the coruscating pulse
of ghost water

grinds its talons
into the graveled bed's
dry skeleton

The brightwinged spirit
hurls itself
into opaque memory
ossified at the instant
of descent

Opus Six

Stars rise
dragging up the abandoned
glide of a black snake's
delicate bones

wavering through the darkness
the brilliance of tunneled canyon

Opus Seven

restless subterranean waters
clutch their secrets
their quiet knowledge
as they huddle
against a stone heartbeat

Opus Eight

Lightning
through a cloud wrack
the unexpected
flashbraided with
blinding illumination

a moment of time
permanented
through its spot weld
to a molten particle
of space

Opus Nine

Beneath the thunderwatered
uplands
a sigh

bones of the earth
and the creatures
who crept our lives
forward

asleep at the bottom
of time's vault

glimpsed
in the moment
between memory and respiration:
harbinger and revenant

for Tom Auer
1953-2003

Black Snake

... not to Earth confined
But sometimes in the Air
Juan el Grande, PL, V, 78, 79

Crickets in the brome
The wind's voice
in sun and shadow

A mourning dove
pleads with the heat
the sky in its whimper

In the darkness of God's mind
an owl calls the moon
to bleed its golden mist
through a wrack of cloud branches
into the peppergrass husks

Dry needles rustle
as the world curls in
upon itself

A limber pine's roots
stand out of a torn earth

The mouse's shining eyes
the brilliance of a tiny heart
the rush of wing and wind and shadow
the spiral into *bright essence,*
darkness visible

Duende

A river's secret twin, a ghost of air
True History of the Kelly Gang
—Peter Carey

A washing shadow rides night currents
above the breathing river.

Great cottonwoods line the banks
motionless as stalks
of summer's dried cheatgrass.

A waterfall of moonlight crashes
and spumes, yellow moths and fireflies
swim the pale spectre,

nighthawks bullroar the mirage
like death angels bearing messages
of futility and deception.

The living water cuts the hills
toward western canyons through wild nights
strewn with huge stones,
then drowns in shimmering miles of sand

and the wind peels away
the ghost of river
with its gnarled fingers

and the moon pulls its long roots back
through the hardscrabble crust of cloud
into clear sky. The sweet scent

of smouldering starlight wafts
through the hollow
between dream and reality,

harmony's secret gateway
lowers on imperceptible draw ropes.

Nocturne   Sliver Moon   Datura

In the tightest quiet
a sound of glistering.
A fragrance trapped within
the opening bud,
the breath of a night
without a yesterday or tomorrow.
The desert under
a piece of sharp light,
a shard of windstone
broken off the moon
hides its tangled dreams
inside the bone white blossom.

THREE

We are but pigmies lost among the boulders
—John Wesley Powell

the quiet sentience of rock
—Jacqueta Hawkes
A Land

The summit of
Mount Everest is marine limestone
—John McPhee
Basin and Range

Autumn   Wind   Song

—after Bunya No Asayasu

Hanging dew
undried in the eaves
sings through the window,
the scattered jewels
of a broken necklace.

Autumn Koan

Until the path unspooled its way
between blue granite pillars
and dark pine
to the place where shovels
full of sunlight pour in sluices
scented like ripe pear
the great waterfall
uttered no sound.

Suddenly a trough of thunder,
a sodden roar wrapped in bolts
of blue winding sheet:
the secret drum of the forest's heart
or the drenched kindling stone
of gravity and rushing water
or the sudden and terrifying
voice of God?

—for Eleanor Rand Wilner,
homage

Stephen Dedalus on the Slide Guitar

John 1:5

Darkly they are there
behind this light,
darkness shining
in the brightness.

Saturated with solitude
they paint portraits
of the canyonland curvature
on their scalloped underbellies.

Their mysterious migration,
the rhythmic motion
mirrors scarp and basin,
fragments of the earth's breakup,

then slowly rises,
moves like shades
across outer boundaries
into the heaventree of stars

hung with humid
nightblue fruit.

Frost Warning

Stars crowd the sky,
hollows between its branches flare
like a stallion's nostrils
taking air

sharp in moonlight

rimed arête
framed
in night's windshear

★   ★   ★

Cold gusts scud
their mulberry fragrance
like midnight's manada

Joy as crisp breeze
breaks through the stockade,
freed from the flame clotted mirage
of underworld

down the Henrys

Silence trails
while brooding thunderheads,
sepulchered,
await resurrection

* * *

A falling star
sheds its sparks
into dark wake

flowing mane
quavering hoofmarks
of squall line

A chilled wind racks
through the Comb Wash
gauntlet of red stone

chases spooked mare's tails
across the desert sky

Thornapple Aubade

In one vision of heaven, a childhood village,
no roads enter or leave,
measured streets, white dwellings, sparkling
windows mirror the clean visage of fair folk

in another, mountains blue as the virgin's serape,
broken stone, arroyos and slot canyons, honeycombed
forests cradle a still pond, turquoise,
a silver gleam in an emerald mount

then a beachscape stippled and golden,
waves white and wild as the eyebrows of God
or calm and silky as a wolf's trailing bellyfur
or the feathery lace of sunwarmed moss

perhaps a wildflower filled canoe dream,
its fire opal breast, invokes winddrift
with mottled green wings, its beating heart
flurries eternal tides

or quiet cloisters where shadows breathe
tomed solitude, candlelight eddy
sifts moondrenched gaps
between the intuitions of darkness and night

or, finally, eternal
                    dreamless
           unbroken
               sleep

Requiem
Sonata for Ellen

The human spirit, it is said, yearns for glimpses into the
"interiority" of a being that is different, not us, something
not quite comprehensible, something that moves in its own
complete universe.

Ellen Meloy
1946-2004

Sunrise: *Andante*

> *A band of sky so vibrant in its blue,*
> *it is neither space nor air,*
> *but silence become matter*

Eastern mesas glow
in the vanishing darkness
like campfire embers

Henry laccoliths
grip the drift net of sky,
a thin elbow of cloud propped
where the waning Hunter's moon
belies rumors of its exile
then slides into the darkness of sleeve

slips of light
squirm through rips
like gashes of falling water

The cloud trails
one smoking wing,
a snapped branch,
over the desert

morning star
a point of white fire
limning the mesa

A cholla stretches its fingers
scrawls petroglyphs
into sky,
lost herds,
wandering bighorns
search for the blue door
hidden beneath
the purple desert varnish
of dawnseep

       ★   ★   ★

A low mist of light
spreads a stain
over the desert,
bulges, exhales,
slides into cobalt sky

All the wind's edges
honed fine
carve sweeping flairs
from shy spirit shadows
of abandoned cloud

heat already rises
from cracks where earth
was yanked out
from beneath itself,
thermals slicing the thick air
into a serpentine mirage
of prowling currents

Creosote nod at the mesa,
whisper
the tenor of today's wind

     ★   ★   ★

A lone juniper
trapped in the gap
between mesas

Sunlight rains through
like the flap of a blazing
prayer flag

the cholla, silver,
framed,
a glittering menorah

Eaton's penstemon,
blossoms like closed bells
hold in sound,

scarlet Buddhas
joying in limitation
pour like lava

A raven's rusted voice,
plangent, nailed
into a truss of morning

Light spills
through liquid silence
of a heliotrope sky

sluices of aspen gold
wash the crimson slickrock

Midday: *Adagio*

coruscated shafts of winter sunlight

Mesa and arch
transept and flying buttress
under a corn flower sky
the color of heaven

a red tail hawk
wind drifts,
disappears
into a fold of stone
then floats out
of a hanging arroyo
suspended like a hammock
in the bluff wall

splintered light
shales and marls
jade and turquoise

      ★   ★   ★

clastic dikes,
the desert's red bones
exposed,
earth's skin
ripped and peeled away
by a malpais talon

sun's breath
leaks into grabens
and basins

slot canyons
fill with the seep
of red and golden light
as if ringing gusts
moved through flames

a day orphaned
from its season
so hot rocks spall
great rumbling slabs
exorcised demons twisting
in the blistered air

     ★   ★   ★

Beneath white washed
Navajo cliffs
a horned rattlesnake
crawls into a cactus shadow

Like a starving wraith
a roadrunner
stalks the gleam
of windscoured sand,
his beak a scythe rising
and falling in the sharp light

     ★   ★   ★

A small cloud
wilts
in sunbleached sky
shadows meshing

the waltz
of a painted lady
butterfly

harbinger of rain
or earthquake or
fire or silence
or wind or
drought

flutters into an arroyo
stretching down cracked earth,
traces ancient storm trails
to mounds of sunlight shards
crammed and tamped
in canyon bottoms

grottos and hoodoos,
smooth bowls holding
bighorned anthropomorphs,
dancing gods
hiding among
gnarled twists of stone
like niched saints
in La Sagrada's adobe walls

Evening: *Allegretto*

> *The rescue line comes from*
> *intimate witness to nature's*
> *genius, to the pure facts of*
> *the non-human lives that*
> *are still possible in this far-*
> *off desert.*

A small cloud
clings to the edge of a bluff,
peers over horizon
rises with thermals
swelling
its bloated darkness

crawls into bluebird sky
like a penitente wrapped in the net
of a black shawl

sky enameled
by the churn of gathering cumulus
thickens and grumbles

while the earth
slides
on its journey

     ★   ★   ★

Duskwind stoops
and scrapes up
a fistful of sand,
tosses it into air

82

sky shifting vermilion,
creosote nods
like Pampas grass

    ★   ★   ★

Behind the Henrys
lightning the shape of snake dreams
uncoils in molten twilight,
grafted to horizon
tongues lick the air,
lacing the sky
a distant rumble
like the faint peal
of earth's plates
deep
below the canyon's belly

    ★   ★   ★

Warm rain
sings like pebbles,
trickles down
a slickrock chute
into a sandstone bowl

earth steams
with scent of juniper
and sage,
damp adobe

tinajas fill
with the dance of raindrops
splashing like children

shy whisper and mumble
as a small rivulet
rushes through sand and cheatgrass
last splinters
of rain captured sunlight
linger
in piñon needles

      ★   ★   ★

The rising moon
pretends to sulk
behind dark cuestas

reappears in the gap
between the open lips
of Butler Wash,
Kokopelli's flute
lifted to thin
jorobado light

their reflection
red and gold
in the brown San Juan

      ★   ★   ★

a shaft of moonlight
clear as the flesh of a spectre

or a wandering god

Coda: Midnight: *Troppo Sotto Voce*

> *Is it the winter's stillness,*
> *where the loudest sound is silence,*
> *that makes it so?*

A single windhowl cuts through night's coils
like a hound's belling

before the lightning shattered shelter
of a broken heart

Clouds lash the fading Hunter's moon
with silver laced thorns

A braided web of stars
holds up the river of sky

like the nets used to capture
painted wings and great mountain sheep

petroglyphs etched
upon the heart's canyon walls

then released as flecks of ash
into cooling air

drift from the fire ring
into the flight of ravens

distant as the memory of thunder
or close as midnight's stillness

—for Mark Meloy

85

Equinox   Novena

...the future has already passed, many times, and around lie the ruins of old futures dreamed.

—Tony Cohan, *On Mexican Time*

At the stone cuesta's
bent knees
a boulder graveyard

★　★　★

This rock choked slot
carved
by an ancient river

★　★　★

Dried streambed cottonwoods
shiver, their minds
focusing color explosions

★　★　★

Afternoon mirage
bends a cañoncito upward,
hanging in air

★　★　★

Rabbit brush waft
gold
as a cloistered god's ransom

★　★　★

A blue glow,
cool dusk shadows
wander the arroyos

   ★   ★   ★

Nightwind's shush
fills the space
between twilight and moonrise

   ★   ★   ★

A bloated third quarter moon
purls
into eastern shallows

   ★   ★   ★

Mars
like an orphan coal
above the Fisher Towers

Sabbath Year, Insomnia

Afternoon. Cicadas drum
their rattling vigil, a scream
in the brain. The pain
a thorn or a serpent's fang feels
entering the flesh of God.

Shed skins cling to tree bark
in their liquid rustle,
like the memory of a child's coat
on a cedar post or mesquite limb
waiting for the owners to return,
then disappear in gyres of wind.

Evening, a Palmer's penstemon horizon
made of sound, a pale pink
underlaid with brilliant globe mallow.
The wistful colors of love and courage
call Orion to come forth,
elbow on the moon, and lean
toward the desert.
Shadows crawl the humming
branches of midnight.

Venus paling flees the grit of light
as it crawls over the La Sals. Morning song,
a kind of holiness, a reminder
of our impermanence: a brief fragrance,
the bloom of an evening primrose,
a sunrise felt clearly, once,
a thrum in the cottonwoods
that continues after the senses fold
their petals and begin the dream of sleep.

November Idyll

after the still life
—Leviticus 7:12-15

Above the grain field stubble
a lift of cranes

like a great table cloth
shaken

Windburst

Into the crushed purple sage scent
of a pungent afternoon sky
crisp as the brief memory
of a newly dreamed god
an innocent cloud
yucca blossom creamy
scuds against a cedar waxwing's
rising trill

Suddenly a devil gyre
fallen through a crevice
in the sky pours
its nine tailed scream
upon a juniper
straining against its roots
like a tethered foal

flings its arms outward,
huge scoops of wind hurled
against the mesa abutment,
sand explosions spurt
like torn sheets of flame,
burst into afternoon
in a bellow of celebration,
a whiplash cavern
the wind rushes through

drops into an arroyo
Creosote branches flail
like the thin arms of a maestro
calling forth a Beethoven huzzah

then relax as if a ghost's hands
shook the limbs,
slowly moves away

Suspended in the gap
between the mind of wind
and the mind of stone
a wayward cottonwood leaf,
sojourner on a tendril of air,
winds itself around
a slickrock fin,
searches the wind's self portrait
carved in sand
for the cool embrace
of quiet shadow
to sleep the sleep of seeds
patiently biding
the vicissitudes of time

Cold Snap

coldness and delay
—Shakespeare, *Othello* II. iii, 388

Dusk submerged
in a sage
perfumed novena
melts into wisps of air,
a gold powder
filters through buttes
and towers,
embraced against the earth
by the press of starlight

Sudden freeze,
an invisible wall
stacked and mortared
on the footings of space
and time, afternoon's
molten air fragile
and metallic;
the desert tightens,
snaps with a touch

Light honed
to an eye pouring white
as the texture
of green implodes,
snags blood red
on mesas and piñons,
casts twilight shadows
long and sharp edged
as scythes

The rising moon of falling leaves
inflamed,
canyon wrens
sing siren songs

Nocturne   Chinle Strata

An immense, rainbow colored intaglio
—Wallace Stegner, *Beyond the Hundredth Meridian*

A small cloud hangs above the mesa
Shadows crawl down the escarpment

La Tierra turns
and afternoon slides toward dusk

Sage brush winds
cool the evening air

A day passes into week
month, year, century, millennium, eon

Pangaea splits into continents
which float, collide, grind, erupt

Sierras thrust against the sky
wash to the seas

Civilizations spawn, rise
fall into blackbird gurgle

The desert glistens under a quarter moon
dangling like a question mark

hooo hooo
—a long eared owl, slicing
silence

94

Tumbleweed: an Autumn Portrait

—for Bob Nolan, "slowly moving...drifting"

Heat waves
rooted in the depth of canyon
rise like a taut lattice
of desiccant run off,
lift the equinox desert
into air

A small black cloud
lost in the flyways
folds over a pivot of sky,
collapses into itself, a crested breaker
tossed against the splintered light,
vanishes

Great slabs and boulders,
collapsed buttresses
fallen into a relict cemetery,
an askew breastwork
circling an abandoned cathedral
surrounds the sunwrenched butte

Twisted cholla
blistered into gnarled grotesques
glow like revenant martyrs
staggering toward twilight,
embrace each other,
cling to the desert's crust

A tumbleweed cloaked in wind
moves like time,
respecting neither geography,
beginning, nor end,
sojourns the dried earth,
a wraith with apostate faith

scatters its seed,
rolling on its own skeleton
toward the long, open
midnight of solstice,
black as the portals
of eternity

Moon of the Hummingbird

Genesis 32:23-32   Hebrews 11:1-3   Darwin 14
Goosenecks, San Juan River

This silver light
like drips of memory
between the slot canyon walls
of belief and impermanence

We glide
through the double-sided mirror
our minds name in whispers
the watery gate to heaven
in our glass bottomed rafts
of dreamlight

the Cyclops eye we approach
a round self-portrait
shaped by the insistence of faith,
arrogance
and our imagined gods' hands

The bright white gleam
in the hollowed thigh
of Jacob's night

blossoms in the wake
of tiny wings
thrumming the air
as they gather
to the flyways of geese

We left adrift and crippled
in the waters of night

flotsam

carried to primordial shore
supine
and dried silver
by moonlight

Moon   Wind   Owl

The moon slipped
from its thin shelf of cloud

holds the pond
mirror still
under the chill stare
of an owl's eye
with its pressing weight

A lift of nightwind
soughs in the juniper
then drops with the rustle
of scuttling mice
into the scramble
of manzanita

The dark bird
scoops its wings
full with air

with the gravity hunger
of a falling stone

plunges
into the silence
of shadow

FOUR

The earth does not belong to us.
We belong to the earth
—Chief Seattle

The world is full of gods
—Thales

Such a price the gods exact for song,
to become what we sing
—Goethe

Idyll

Michael Haydn, Horn Concerto in D major

Sky reverberates
with the smudge of cranes

Their gabble
thaws the clumsy thickness
of winter soaked morning

Cold Star Wind Sonatina

Just before sunrise
a scruffy little chill
trailing clumps of bellyfur
slinked into a hollow,
sniffed out a burrow
between the creosote,
twined into its tail three times
and lay down
peering through half closed eyes
at the eastern mesa glowrim

a dark bluff
and Venus glimmering,
silver moon
pales above

From an arroyo
a small wind creeps
through prickly pear,
surrounds a dark juniper
then writhes itself into a dirndl

sand, leaves, twigs
embrace in the mottled air
then fling apart
like a shattered covey
of Gambel's quail,
float across pale sand,
drop into earthcracks
and seepholes,
vanish

In the empty space
carved by the dust devil
raddled strands of morning light
rise, shimmer
and stretch
beneath mother sky

Matins in the Cathedral of Wind

> If I stay here long enough
> I will learn the art of silence.
> After I have given up words
> I will become what I have to say.
> —Richard Shelton, "Desert"

If I stay here long enough
in this havoc of landscape,
colloquy where enormous rocks
collapse into each other,
this place of desert and sky
wrenched apart by stone walls
buttressed with crimson arches,
shafts of light or brilliant clefts
suddenly opened with a hush
like the quickly drawn breath
of ancient winds trapped
in cool silence of primordial dunes
pressed into stone, where
a rough-legged hawk rides wind drift
in a lazy helix, waits
for rising thermals above the
tortured wreckage of sand
and stone, creosote and desert phlox,
sky and jagged horizon, each
glimpse, touch, scent its own
mélange of belief,
trinity of grace, beauty, dignity

will I learn the art of silence
and through silence hear breath
from another world cross and spill

over the juncture, sough as the moon
folds its wings and rests
on the shadow of a limned bluff,
arroyos echo the deafening roar
as starlight tunnels its way
into labyrinth and from that echo
understand there are no geographies
in the language of man
whereby one may find wisdom,
only to live here long enough
in this most sacred of sanctuaries
and learn not silence
but the art of silence
and the knowledge there is
no art without faith in existence,
that frail detritus of belief,
or believing in belief,
the intersection between
stone and wind, light and shadow,
no more than a tatter of cloud
caught on a ragged bluff's selvage
in this valley of kings where
the sojourner lingers until

after words have been given up
like flung jewels stitched into clouds
where strands of sunlight glitter
in the La Sal's snow wedges,
now lifted by a wind tendril
into a flood of rushing light
westward like thunder to smash
against the Moab red wall
as it blisters the darkness
into trembling fingers of shadow
clinging to any rock crevice,

then scrapes downward
until all is ablush, as if God
slapped the desert's face
into brilliance, horizon
suddenly broken as arroyo
winds into absence of canyon
where earth fell
into a hollow beneath itself,
the world alive with the gift
of light: cloud shadows
race westward, up the mesa walls,
angle north, then leap
the horizon beyond sight;
cool silence of a salt dome,
the braided persimmon moon fragrance
lingering in beardtongue, peppergrass
and yucca, the bend of sunlight
into open lip of slot canyon,
manifestation of *beresith*,
the great command *let there be*
hurled into the void of darkness
until word became flesh
and drew first breath
of crimson wind and world
became living sanctuary,
body of divinity manifest,
the words given up,
transformed into most holy
of holies whispering through the wind

I become what I have to say
sunlight bent and cooled
by the flow into seep rock
inside the lip of slot canyon,
walls scoured clean by wind,

where glistens the amazing
white flower of sacred datura,
the burning bush,
a lingering votive candle
held in the open palm
of God's mind.

for the Utah Chapter of
The Nature Conservancy

Wild Rose Nocturne
Wood Flute Sonata

Low dove coo, echo.
The desert's smooth flank.

A soft dipping wind
soaked with sage

pours
a spiral staircase

for darkness.
The great mesa

with night creeping
over its shoulder

and the huge, lovely sprawl
of sand.

Red rock, crimson moon,
copper rose sky.

Turquoise Elegy

> that double-headed monster of salvation and damnation, Time
> —Samuel Beckett, *Waiting for Godot*

I

A hoary bifurcated cottonwood
like a dowsing stick
divines the banshee winds

as they snuff and root
its discalced corpse

then dive
into the labyrinth of cheatgrass
to search out ballast

2

Wrapped in a viuda's shawl
the hag fingered windcoils

howl like a band
of holy and ancient

wrinkled mourners
anticipating obsequies

3

A crippled cholla,
its crumbled shadow twisted
against the crush of twilight

horizon's shoulders
tensed before the sliver moon's
flint edge

the rim of sky shaved
while dusk
shrieks, its tether chain

torn loose
drags in
the dark vast

Eventide
Sunglint   Tree   Hawk

fast falls the eventide
—-Henry F. Lyte

The sun ties
a sheepshank
behind a bowline

to a juniper belay
rimrocked on
a mesa snarl

below
a hovering
vulture

who rides the blaze
wound
of imploding sky

as it tenses
its coppershine
tether

The knot
collapses
to a fist

as
he
rappels

the
glimmer
line

then dissolves
into horizon's
clutch

Thornapple Nocturne

in a vision once I saw
—Coleridge, *Kubla Khan*

Vespers

Holes in the wind gnawed by cactus
Pock scars holy carrion birds
float through like smoky mist

then rise as scythes,
folds sliced in the bright web of air,
leakage of darkness unraveling

Sunset Interlude

The white flower death song
of cloistered light
lodged beneath deep mesas

whirls blowfoot wind
into ash silence,
cataracts the bloodshot eyes

of horizon
Twilight perfectly blends
into mottled shroud, rises

like a manes over the slickrock kiln
Embers of collapsing heaven
sluice into earth's open vault,

all the sails of sandgrain dust
still before time's crypt

Compline

A shaft of dusklight
bright as a self-immolated nun
flings into air,

wilts into cloven carapace,
melts to icedream
puddles of smoke and nightshade

The moon, like Lazarus, comes forth
to embrace the joy of white blossom

Desert   Moon   Star

the dark night of the soul
—San Juan de la Cruz

Slicing the synapse
between horizon
                and mesa
a half moon
thin and silver
as the severed wing
of a lost
            and abandoned
fallen angel's ghost.
The miracle of quiet
a trick
        to remind us
of its presence
as when
            a shooting star
shishes between anvil
                and stirrup
in the mind's ear
and the residue of its memory
                    crackles.

Wind   Sand   Moon   Arch

A small nightwind
sleddog tired
from pulling
on the sunset's traces,

a whirl of sand
as it burrows
into the desert's
skeleton, searching
for the pelvic opening.

Dusk shadows
crawl out of arroyos,
from behind boulders
and juniper,
begin
their shy slink
across sand,
up the bajadas.

A crack
in the cloud
spills planed curls
of moonsliver,
opens,

creosote arms
panhandle starlight.

Landscape arch
a thin glisten

in the spiraling glow,
the hollow
black

as a workshop wall's
painted outline,
a borrowed
Swede saw

taken
and unreturned,
an old dog's dreamyelp
for a lost bone

covered
by the drifting
sand.

Mind Drift: Neolithic Sliver Moon

Caminante, no hay camino
Se hace camino al andar
 —Antonio Machado

I

A young moon at twilight
prowls its haptic way across
the belly of fifty mile mountain

sharpens its horns
on the bark
of a perfectly cloudless night

the desert warm, nacreous
in dim glow

soft whir of a swallow
stitching the selvage of starlight

cricket song

wind whistle of bat flight

2

A viejo moon, macerated, antlers nub dulled,

stoop shouldered and humpbacked

the rabbit long ago
caught and eaten

hobbles between hummocks
into the alleyway of horizon

back turned to Ishtar,
the affair a barmecide feast,
suspended, gone

she, irreverent as a waking jay,
across the sky, above Kaiparowits
welcomes sun

Century Plant
Wind   Moon   Owl

> The darkness drops again
> —Yeats, "The Second Coming"

1

South wind moves
through a slash of cross timbered sandstone
and hoodoos like castaway burls
awaiting the pyre

under a waning quarter moon
snagged on a barb
in the horizon

empties itself
into the valley
of exhumed catacombs
channeling thin light
into the desert's exhausted wellspring

2

Cougarwind slinks
across the bajada
slices down a fault
and drops
into a gash of cañoncito

a serpentine cat's cradle
seeps away
like thought
into the clutch
of a Jungian death demon

3

Curled parchment
four-winged saltbush
rattles in the wind
as it searches
for a desiccated vision
to inflict on a dying pariah

an agave nearing the moment of death
in full twenty foot bloom
sacrifices its timelessness
to the moon's point of reference

this noneternal moment
of rising personal significance

the ultimate fragility

panicle of burst pods
rattle like arthritic knuckles
on a hallowed anchoress
counting prayer beads
between exequies

4

a martyr
gone to shelter
beneath a bloodshot sky

within a great fortress
of cactus and stone

death leers
over the bastions

the wind spirals

5

An owl's rusted voice
nailed by the moon
into a cross truss of sky

A white feather
curled upon wind drift sand

for Bill Holm
1943-2009

Dark of the Moon

after Tsurayuki

A star emerges from the blackness
begins its quiet journey
rowing the dark river of sky

A mourning dove whimpers,
its recollection an edge of dream
meant left forgotten

A silence deep as an owl's flight,
a lone snowflake falls
from an obsidian heaven

Winter Solstice
Moon   Night   Desert

1

Scabland. Sere.
The mesa top pressed flat
by the blue weight of sky,
its gnarled sides
sunsucked crimson.

Yesterday's moon
drowned
in an ocean of canyon,
today's desert sunclotted.

2

Afternoon,
the turbid intimacy
of tattered low hanging clouds,
tangle of cross breeze. Evening,
shreds of late light
snag in the cholla's outstretched arms.

Wind, rock, light and time
form a hinge and fold over
into themselves.

3

The shy sleepiness
of a thin mesquite shadow
in an aging twilight,

bajada
flat on its back,
awake.

The rimrocked moon,
astride the cuesta
trembles, rises in a silver shimmer

as a passing of starlight over water
into the dark chamber of night,
curtain, mirror and lamp.

Shadows stretch their black fingers
into the pink barranca,
pull themselves forward.

4

This place of sand and rock
with an ocean's memory.

The desert dreams moon,
feels the tide in her belly,
slow rise of great stones.

The moon dreams sea,
neap and ebb,
dance of wave and ripple
sculptured in slickrock

petrified oyster beds
in the escarpment,
primordial fish
frozen in layers of slate

breath of ocean
in a night breeze
wends homeward
through a rock strewn gully

spindrift redolence
upon the face
in an abandoned stream bed

echo of breaking waves
from sandstone labyrinths.

5

The sojourning wind
tethered to a sprawling juniper

moonflooded desert
opalescent
beneath a bright spill of stars

the creosote's uplifted arms
drenched with light.

—for Ken Brewer 1941-2006

Solstice, Midnight

A life is a history of goodbyes.
—Sam Hamill

Paralyzed memory
a dark mist of sorrow
suspended

between absence
and acknowledgement
of the finality of loss

like the first line
of an unaccomplished
fugue

or the abandoned search
for a buried lodestone
moonwrenched almost to light

or inside bloodthrob
dreamed farewells
of southbound passenger pigeons

falling through
crepuscular sky,
a synapse flicker

or an echo
just at the edge
of discernment

On the summit of the opposite wall of the canyon
are rock forms that we do not understand.

—John Wesley Powell

Winter   Morning   Shaving

—after Hitomaro

The house filled
with the moondried
scent of quiet.

A strange old man
startles me,
staring through my mirror.

Notes

"Matins: In the Moonset" was a wedding gift for my children: for Jon and Lynette and for JoDee and Jim

"Mutant Haiku at Ground Zero" is for Terry Tempest Williams; illigitimi non corborundum, m'lady

"Black Snake" is for Chris Faatz and JoDee Ellis

All the italicized quotes in "Requiem" are from Ellen Meloy's posthumous book, *Eating Stone*. This poem was written while I was completing a residency for the Colorado Land Trust in Salida, Colorado.

The italicized quotes in "Stephen Dedalus on the Slide Guitar" are from James Joyce's *Ulysses*.

"Moon of the Hummingbird" is for the Possum, world class moongazer, and was written during a residency sponsored by the New Iberia, Louisiana library, administered by my adopted sister Susan Hestor Edmunds.

"Matins in the Cathedral of Wind" is a variation on Eleanor Wilner's variation of the 15th century Spanish Glosa that she invented and used in her poem "AUTI'O, Cassandra" in her book *The Girl With Bees in Her Hair* (Copper Canyon Press), my personal choice for outstanding book of poetry published in 2004. The poem is dedicated to the Utah Chapter of The Nature Conservancy.

"Eventide" is for world class mountaineer and splendid friend Mikel Vause.

"Desert Moon Star" is for Doña Susan and Don Ricardo of Salida, Colorado.

"Wind   Sand   Moon   Arch" is for Bud.

"Nocturne   Sliver Moon   Datura" is for Michael Donovan

"Wild Rose Nocturne" is for Owl and Evie

A small handful of poems in this manuscript began as exercises in sonnet writing; after writing technically proficient but generally mediocre sonnets, I translated them into Chinese characters, then back into English with, hopefully, a better result. Other poems began as exercises written in Chinese characters, such as "Moon   Wind   Owl," written in the library of the Mountain Writers Center in Portland, Oregon, while I was working during a residency there, and were then translated into English and completed in that language.

Acknowledgments

Poems in this manuscript were first published or anthologized in the following journals or collections: *Annotations, Ash Canyon Review, Bare Root Review, City Art, Ellipsis, Entrada, Hayden's Ferry Review, Isotope, Oregon Literary Review, Paddlefish, Poetry East, Salt Flats Annual, Sugar House Review, Susan Makov Broadsides, The Manner of the Country: Living and Writing in the American West, Utah Sings, Wasatch Journal, Weber Studies, Willow Springs Magazine.*
"November Idyll" was first published in *Orion.*
"Century Plant" was first published in *Isle.*

The author wishes to thank Eleanor Wilner, Michael Donovan, Rob Van Wagoner, Ruth Lee, Alan and Evie, Bill Holm, Barry Scholl and the Entrada Gang, Sam Green, John Lane, Bruce Hucko, Gailmarie Pahmeier and Jan Marie Lee for careful reading, gracious criticism, encouragement, and useful guidance and love songs along the way in the making of this book, and to Sam Hamill for thirty years of being my patient editor and mentor. Thanks also to Susu Knight for the lovely painting used on the cover.

                                   Abrazos y amor a todos.

A NOTE ABOUT THE AUTHOR

David and Jan Lee split time between their home in Bandera, Texas and their R.V. in Seaside, Oregon, where he scribbles and wanders trails and byways, all at about the same rate and pace. In 2003, Lee retired from Southern Utah University, where he received every teaching award given by the institution, including being named Professor of the Year on three occasions. In 1997 he was named Utah's First Poet Laureate, a position he held until 2003. Presently Lee is in intense training to achieve his goal of becoming a World Class Piddler.

·COLOPHON

Designed and produced by Bob Blesse at the
Black Rock Press, University of Nevada, Reno.
The typeface is Quadraat, designed by
Dutch type designer Fred Smeijers,
The display font is Trajan, designed
by former Adobe type designer,
Carol Twombley.
Printed and bound by
Thomson-Shore, Inc.,
Dexter, Michigan.